More Praise for *What Had Happened Was*

"*What Had Happened Was* is a daring poet's debut. First and foremost, I want to praise Therí Alyce Pickens's collection for its unflinching attention to the nuances of—and everyday sorts of elaborate formal play embedded in—African American vernacular. It's truly refreshing, and energizing, to see the dynamism of Black linguistic expression live a full life in contemporary American poetry this way. It's all here. Love and loss, theory and autobiography, the ordinary and the transcendent."—Joshua Bennett, author of *Spoken Word: A Cultural History*

"Few debut poetry books are long awaited. Without a doubt, *What Had Happened Was* is. When you work tirelessly and patiently to master your art—with skill, wisdom, and an abundance of imagination—it reads like this."—Hayan Charara, author of *These Trees, Those Leaves, This Flower, That Fruit: Poems*

"In her constantly surprising and deftly built poems, Therí Alyce Pickens enacts a poetics that refuses binaries, attends to and extends the power of Black art, and centers a body navigating illness. Pickens seamlessly moves through and braids memory, history, pop culture. The language is precise and remarkable; it will engage and entangle you in marvelous ways—as will the formally inventive poems and the structure itself. Pickens has written an electric first book. The poems are still sparking in my mind."—Eduardo C. Corral, author of *Guillotine: Poems*

What Had Happened Was

Duke University Press
Durham and London 2025

What
Had
Happened
Was

Therí Alyce Pickens

© 2025 Duke University Press
All rights reserved
Printed in the United States of America on acid-free paper ∞
Project Editor: Liz Smith
Designed by Dave Rainey
Typeset in SangBleu Republic by Copperline Book Services

Library of Congress Cataloging-in-Publication Data
Names: Pickens, Therí A., author. | Pickens, Therí A.
What had happened was (Poem)
Title: What had happened was / Therí Alyce Pickens.
Other titles: What had happened was (Compilation)
Description: Durham : Duke University Press, 2025.
Identifiers: LCCN 2024024169 (print)
LCCN 2024024170 (ebook)
ISBN 9781478031499 (paperback)
ISBN 9781478028284 (hardcover)
ISBN 9781478060505 (ebook)
Subjects: LCGFT: Poetry.
Classification: LCC PS3616.I276 W44 2025 (print) |
LCC PS3616.I276 (ebook) | DDC 811/.6—dc23/eng/20241105
LC record available at https://lccn.loc.gov/2024024169
LC ebook record available at https://lccn.loc.gov/2024024170

long story short

this is for anybody

who would be one

of my little friends

Variety, multiplicity, eroticism are difficult to control. And it may very well be that these are the reasons why writers are often seen as *persona non grata* by political states, whatever form they take, since writers/artists have a tendency to refuse to give up their way of seeing the world and of playing with possibilities; in fact, their very expression relies on that insistence. Perhaps that is why creative literature, even when written by politically reactionary people, can be so freeing, for in having to embody ideas and recreate the world, writers cannot merely produce "one way."

Barbara Christian, "The Race for Theory"

What good is any form of literature to Black people?

What good is science fiction's thinking about the present, the future, and the past? What good is its tendency to warn or to consider alternative ways of thinking and doing? What good is its examination of the possible effects of science and technology, or social organization and political direction? At its best, science fiction stimulates imagination and creativity. It gets reader and writer off the beaten track, off the narrow, narrow footpath of what "everyone" is saying, doing, thinking—whoever "everyone" happens to be this year.

And what good is all this to Black people?

Octavia E. Butler, "Positive Obsession"

I like to use poems as what-if machines and as time-traveling devices, and I'm grateful to have had the chance to do that with this project. I learned a lot, and I hope you learn something too and then go tell someone else about it.

Eve L. Ewing, *1919*

I put a hunnit percent in every line I drop.

Lil' Kim, "Quiet Storm (Remix)"

CONTENTS

THIS

2	On This Day
3	The Amateur Gardener Considers a Time of Death
5	*On March 12, 2020, Breonna Taylor*
6	On Losing; a Hypothesis
7	Customary Calculus for Chronicity
9	Getting Dressed
10	*Depression*, Jacob Lawrence, 1950
11	*If Lyndon B. Johnson hadn't had his heart attack*
12	*Remember the episode of* Bones *when*
13	Ode to Checking My Shit
15	Anatomy of Soap
17	*my lover says (my mind)*
18	*I found out I have something*
19	Ursa Corregidora and Mary J. Blige Contemplate Life without Children

THAT

22	Dispatches from the Pediatric Floor
23	Collar Is What Hangs around the Neck
25	*I am watching a documentary about food, again*
26	Corona Poem
27	*T*
28	On sex
29	Palimpsestina
31	The Amateur Gardener Contemplates Trauma

32	Apostrophe to Inspiration
34	Chronically Ill
35	On recompense
36	*I tell her some of her ancestors must have snitched on Harriet Tubman*
37	What You Don't See When Ben Vereen Guest Stars as Will's Father on *The Fresh Prince*, May 1994

MIND YOU

40	What Had Happened Was

& THE THIRD

56	Variation on a Theme
57	Potential Ode or Elegy Out My Window
58	Neighborhood Watch
59	Coming Home
61	Ranunculus
62	*It was just before Thanksgiving*
63	June 2018
64	Ursa Corregidora Goes to Junior High in the 1990s
65	Some Suicides Are Slow
67	*I got into a Twitter beef with Lolo Jones over a blind white girl*
68	What Cliff Should Have Told Theo on the Pilot of *The Cosby Show*, September 1984
70	*Antony and Cleopatra*, dir. Simon Godwin, National Theatre, 2019
72	*my lover says (he doesn't remember)*
73	*I meet a man with a stutter*
75	**Let Me Holla at You Right Quick; or Notes**
81	**I Ain't Forget about Y'all; or Acknowledgments**

THIS

On This Day

You were told to delay my birth with chicken noodle soup.
In April that year, they caught the Beauty Queen
Killer. Ronald Reagan still had not said HIV/AIDS.
Vanessa Williams had to give up her Miss America
crown. I would later become a pageant girl.
Those aren't contractions, said the man lying
next to you. My Little Pony was on sale and the radio
played "Do They Know It's Christmas?" too loudly.
Diahann Carroll and Joan Collins were on the cover
of *Jet* magazine in January and Bill Cosby was in August.
I would wear "Jet Beauty of the Week" tees as a joke.
You spent thirty-two hours in labor and then underwent
a cesarean. That summer, the Olympics
were held in LA and the Soviets didn't come.
They were still angry about 1980. The Apple
Macintosh computer went on sale for $2,500.
I bought mine for a song. Tina Turner and Prince
topped the charts with doves and absent love.
It was a Sunday. Big Mama Thornton, Benjamin Mays,
Julio Cortázar, and Michel Foucault all died.
And I would inherit thunder from them.
Jane Austen would have been 209. In English,
I would be the only one to laugh at her jokes.
I have an education and was introduced properly
at 10:37 a.m. in Orange, New Jersey.
It was foggy with 97% cloud cover and a high of 43 degrees.

The Amateur Gardener Considers a Time of Death

with a line from Medora C. Addison's "The Days to Come"

my skittering eyelashes are the first to tell me
I am awake

the flicks of movement, lashes a small curtain
opening to fresh sky

I can hear the fan as it turns
its labored breathing

like the sound of sifting lentils
ritualized music

today I'll uproot and replant
peppers and lemon balm

the greedy squash and tomato plants
steal the light steal the soil

a small rhythm of dig pat dig when uprooting lemon balm
I see the tomato has asserted itself

roots tethered to its softer garden mate
puncturing the soil

the strings tear jaggedly zippering away
I try a gentle uncoupling

for its own good the lemon balm
may die

for their own good the peppers
may die too

I home them in this new earth
scoop the soil near

rub the fissures between their old soil
that is what they knew

and their new home which is to say
the place I hope

they will grow because my hands
have their limits

and no amount of fretting will make the roots
feel less radical

over drizzling rain the fan still going
it is shushing the air

the shower tinkles like a piano on a defunct fuse box
it is stringing me along

back toward the house where now I shall store
my soul with silent beauty

On March 12, 2020, Breonna Taylor

awakened after working
four overnight shifts at the local ER
with its loud flashes and staccato lights—
a hustle she said was going to make 2020
the year of Breonna Taylor—and it is
a beautiful thing that she and Kenny did what all
young couples should get the chance to:
that is, spend the day just chilling,
chat at suppertime over decent barbecue,
that is, the best you can get outside family,
and decide between playing high-stakes UNO
or watching a movie, what all young couples
should get the chance to when they don't choose
and do both as they munch freshly baked cookies
and ice cream, that is, the warm dough hugging
the cold sugar wet, before the movie starts
watching them curled up in bed, and not know
what no young couple should get the chance to,
that is, what interrupts their feeling of *just us*,
what all waits outside their love.

On Losing; a Hypothesis

after Elizabeth Bishop & John Murillo

The science of losing starts with this
hypothesis: just that we been knowing
there is no such thing as whole.

So, lose dignity discreetly, daily. Lose
your clothes in a strip search at the doctor's
office. Leave the shirts with the beautiful

impossible buttons, the pants that zipper,
long sleeves at home. Listen for the missing
words in *I need help*, lists of tasks to complete:

laundry, making groceries, vacation. Let loud
keening scare the passersby with dogs on leashes—
the sound of laughing fit to kill & dressing

to keep from crying. Linger at the lost spaces
of not and undoing. Say word. Curl your
curls around your finger. Lose even the silence

inside your palm, then, let a backbone slip.
The conclusion: to swallow your own tongue
to take care of what's taking care of you.

Customary Calculus for Chronicity

Wake up:

Estimate: <u>what kind of day it will be</u>
   the strength in your hip.

Can you turn over?
Take your meds on time.

Figure: <u>the minutes it takes</u>
   brush your teeth, wash your face, shower.

Will your arms lift high enough today?
Determine the order of operations.

Reduce your labor by half =
rest naked on the towel you placed on the bed =
the chair you put near.

   Count how many minutes before you are late.

Subtract all clothes
$\lim x \to 0 = f$(those that pull over or pull up + all shoes that do not slip on)

You must rotate your bra 180°
by stepping laterally,
grabbing the front,
pinching the back.
Pray.

   The difficulty of this problem is not about pie.

Reduce your labor by half =
rest half-naked on the towel you kept on the bed.

Substitute hoops for posts.

When you contour,
line your face so none
of this lies on the surface
area of your nose.

The point of your cupid's bow
must look as if it is part
of the axis that bisects your whole face.

                                        Count how many minutes before you are late.

The elimination method helps you recognize systems without solution. You need to know before progression. You must learn to express the rate of change to function with independent variables. Derive the limit by calculating how such variables behave.

Getting Dressed

Lime skater dress. Its coral twin with a more daring hemline.
Leather zip-up number that widens my hips to onion curves.
Almost sensible A-line dresses: one with flutter sleeves,
another with a choke collar, a third with ruching from breast to thigh.
ROYGBIV order: frocks from before prednisone stole my style.
I close my closet, sweatshirt in hand.

I pull shapeless cotton over surgical scars:
one from twenty-five years ago when Dr. Forman broke my sternum
in exchange for a bunny beanie baby, one from ten years ago,
and one from three years ago when the nurse saw fit
to hip me to pants without zippers, and last week's.
I tighten my jeans over the dressing.

You have to understand. Now that my ankles resemble can-popped
biscuit dough, I've abandoned my collection of shoes.
Platform oxblood pumps. Studded suede peep-toe booties with spike heels.
Slate and marigold slip-on trainers. I stuff my feet dough
into smart wool socks, my feet into the clogs I know
everyone else bought that year. I am not the only one:

Pissarro worked from a perch in Paris because his eyes let in too much light.
1897 found him in the city when all the others were painting trees and water.
Boulevard Montmartre from a hotel room: he painted Mardi Gras, a morning
with cloudy weather, midday in spring. *The Boulevard Montmartre at Night*.
The city is drenched with light and color, a runway if ever I saw one.

Depression, Jacob Lawrence, 1950

Unlike any hospital wall I've ever known,
the green walls give jello, give vomit chic.
A man with his suspenders, holding his own
hands behind his back, slouches toward
the earth. Another dressed for the cinema,
chin tucked tighter than Waldorf and Statler.
Inside one of the rooms, the light creates angles,
incidence of possibility. Art, they say. Perspective.
In another room, feet turned up toward forever.
At least, it is not forever after. Another kind
of slouching toward the earth. Honestly?
I do not marvel at the man in shit-
colored pajamas, or even the milky pink
coloring all the men in the painting just because

I marvel at the smooth umber hands
that created this portrait of convalescence,
the same ones that hold his glasses or rest
at his temples in photos. He opens his hands in a wing
between hairline and brow, slicing open
places the Met rejected for its *Harlem on My Mind*
exhibit. I do not wonder why he checked
himself into facilities for rest, for exhaustion.
I do not have to. I raise my fingers as if to ask.
His lips hold a sheen saying they've just been licked,
about to tell me. *After all this time*, he murmurs,
I thought we'd be done

If Lyndon B. Johnson hadn't had his heart attack,

the expert says the voting rights act would not have been
signed. Above her head, the picture of MLK and LBJ adjacent
to the picture of Douglass and Lincoln: one man standing
petitioning on the right and the white one seated,
his pen stroking the paper, penetrating ink, changing
the makeup of the world. His word means something
and the other is waiting waiting waiting. LBJ wrote
with his right hand which means the pain jiggered
up his opposite arm and electrified his shoulder first
before it felt like his heart was like the stores on the news,
then the terrible terrible quiet
of not speaking, of not breathing. Others rush
always too slowly, always rather deliberately
to his face, he hears echoing voices from bodies that scurry:
rats finding the place of least resistance or even succor.
In an epiphany he has after nitroglycerin and some rest,
for rest always brings clarity,
he tells the world how to get well again.
He tells the world how to write itself again.
He strokes the pen. He changes the world with his word.
The expert says that was the moment, the exact moment
he knew he needed to act. I heave up from my belly
the air to expel out my nostrils; a gust of wind and water and salt
cleanse the space that holds this story. I too am standing
as best I can in this history. I stood and sat with pens
trying to stroke the world, seduce the words, thrust some sense
into it all. I prick the paper until it bleeds
some precious ink and, at least,
I find empathy without looking in the mirror.*

With a line from Britteney Black Rose Kapri, "othered"

Remember the episode of Bones *when*

Jack was being an asshole in a wheelchair?
Well, I never felt more close to him than then.
This was the guy who understood all there was
to know about soil, silt, particles, chemicals,
and he would never call it dirt. He would never
simplify the complicated. And, here he was felled—
he'd say—by an accident. In ten seasons, nothing else
had injured him permanently: not when his bestie
turned out to be a serial killer, not when he got trapped
by a serial killer, not when the woman he loved refused
to marry him. But this. And, I completely understood
from my own seated perch how he learned to work
the new titanium wheels, how he felt his chest tighten,
the sleekness of biceps aching after a day of living,
living as labor to get around. I can still hear the drone
of the wheelchair lift he used to get to the forensic platform,
the other actresses and actors waiting, his on-screen wife,
Michaela Conlin, with inimitable patience
coaxing him to be the one with the complex answers,
like when I make hard-boiled eggs and peel the shells,
taking flesh into my palm.

Ode to Checking My Shit

after Ross Gay

As I watch nurses
turn their noses up
and CNAs avoid
the conversation with words
never uttered out loud
and ideas only
vaguely gestured at
like they don't know
what I mean
or I don't know
what they mean
and, as doctors never ask,
but I tell them anyway,
I never think to withhold,
to play my vagues,
but rather watch
how color, texture, size
create this moment of recoil.
Sometimes one will admit
they've never heard such detail,
such self-knowledge,
with a straight face
like the years of therapy
paid off,
like the person harangued
for years to pay attention
in her body
finally got it right.
When I peer over the bowl
as though a microscope lay between us—
a set of lenses which
as at the ophthalmologist's

tell me better or worse
or about the same—
I straighten my back
and curve my smile
several times a day
and watch the small islands
settle like Atlantis must have
housing whole worlds
of tiny organisms and the detritus
that used to be food
and sometimes still is.
I make sure to note
how I unload
these burdens
whether it takes the shape
where it now lives
in the S-bend
or if it is like it used to be
a scattered shot in the dark,
rushed to
and screaming with electricity
or if it feels empty
like when it used to come unbidden
into a bag. I relish
the candle doing its work
cleansing the air
setting fire to some evidence
that I lived
but not the moment of relief
to look back
at what I consumed
and let go
thinking maybe there's something
worth savoring.

Anatomy of Soap

let us have all the cakes smooth in their dryness
the imprint of a dove on top   another logo

telling its origin story as a whole food   sometimes
there is no image no writing

to tell us it is natural it is safe
and it did not harm anyone

at first the top layer comes off   teasingly flimsily
slimy   silly   between the tented arch of my thumb

& the voracious whorls of my fingers   i add more water
rub this slice into my hands   leaving it bubbling on a dish

an exciting melting sliding into the sink   faucet off
i slide the slick on my palms   five seconds

cuff one wrist and turn like a doorknob   five seconds
then the other   another five seconds   i lace one set of fingers

over the other coerce the dirt from webbing i use to swim
five more seconds   repeat   five

curve my hands into a finger puppet   eat the opposite palm
nails as dentition   again   ten seconds

rub all over   let the basic lye bind with grit
and whatever else   go running down the drain

the film left feels opposite of clean   but after repeated use
the bar crumbles & i can feel

the oil doing its work   soap is basically a lye
oil and water   you knew that

when i blow   bubbles the light catches the oil
slick inside   the water and the lye bringing them together

my lips forcing my diaphragm to meet my lungs
an unreturned kiss becoming a rainbow

bubbles cluster mid-sky   trusting the air
as they go so fragile a slight wind could   break them

some linger taut and thickened   the audacity of their survival
those float into another becoming   when the bar is close

to halfway used the suds start to feel like rubbing
thick cloth between your hands

washing and drying become the same question
a wet squish's sucking sounds   such a series of small kisses

you can wash your mouth out with it   only now
can you use it over the rest of you   to get clean

only now can you trust the boundedness   two
ingredients that only combine under certain circumstances

when the cake has thinned to communion wafer size
or chunked itself into pieces   let it dry out

and when a few used chips clink like sequestered quarters
you will wonder whether to bind them with the lye you know will hold them

my lover says

my mind is a wilderness and he gets lost in it
sometimes an enjoyable stroll then chaos
he loses track of time in the trees
but I am full of recurring images
recursive scripts that generate more scripts
some an enjoyable stroll then chaos
I found him sitting there at the base of an oak
in my mind the leaves fluttering above him
music over a temperate breeze
and he asked me what's it like in here all the time?
and I said I don't know
only you know the way in
I only know the way out

I found out I have something

in common with Mitch McConnell:
the two of us share a childhood friend,
the kind that binds to the limbs
and constricts our rights
to stretch toward the sun
or, more precisely outlined,
it is the friend that comes stealth
and slow
and sidles like a whisper on the neck,
a grim reaper. Not like death per se
but a curling away from other people,
or really just the people not like us.
We were children: bird-chested and soprano-
voiced, silent before striking out,
silent before becoming preternaturally
mature. That is, we were not children.
The pediatric ward is the killing floor;
the pediatric ward was a floor for congress:
where new ideas sometimes die.
But Mitch and me, the two of us,
share this one secret,
learned in the heat of childhood illness:
survive, honey. Survive.

Ursa Corregidora and Mary J. Blige Contemplate Life without Children

after Tyehimba Jess's leadbelly

                                 I'm good   I'm fine
letting this living seep out my throat   singing
                    I am everything   it is all I ever wanted
the lights the crowd the pulse of it   the microphone is my lover
               the music calls to me   inside me
                from my sacred space   I am choosing me
                          to make generations
            tell me what I ought to do   go on duplicating myself
                          at twilight   in the morning
I don't sing to be supported I sing   I stretch my hands
                        to touch myself   to hold what I alone can possess
                my own piece of ass   my own history they call misery
                the sovereignty of my voice
                           I let it rise   I ride it
                                a beat   steady and thrumming
                                a song   strapped to an untethered balloon
                                          free

THAT

Dispatches from the Pediatric Floor

The nurses' station lights up with computer blue light, women
in brightly colored scrubs flitting from file to patient, hummingbirds
following an arc of perfumed air. Doctors in suits & white coats refuse
to wear sensible shoes, making their presence heard, chart in hand, click
clacking down the hallway. A noise the pediatric ward recognizes
as either mom or physician. I keep my curtain drawn, door closed.
I prefer the quiet, the doctor who wears sneakers.

                                                          My companions:
the cancer girls with their scarves & specially knit blankets & frequent
visitors; the boy band member look-alike who pops wheelies in his new chair;
& the terribly mean Richard whose scowl puts fear into orderlies & his mother.
A preteen fresh out of surgery, I observe most of the day with a mild disinterest,
choosing instead to blink slowly at Richard who, God only knows why, has taken
an intense liking to me. He rides next to me gossiping about our therapist.
She put me in time-out, he whispers hoarsely, *I just ran away*. Punctuating
his freedom, he blows into the tube that controls his chair, doing circles around me.
See? I smirk, the under-eighteen's pact of approval & silence.

                                     Next to him, I breathe steadily, deliberately, wincing. I clutch
the rails of the wall, lock my knees, hoping the mechanics of bone will override muscle
weakness. This terrible business of waiting to fall, waiting to be caught,
will recur well into adulthood; I learn how to grasp the nearest sturdiness.
I learn how to fail at standing up.

                                      I didn't know I could call out, so I begin
my slow descent. Richard is oblivious in his eight-year-old wheeled glory,
still twirling. *See?* I am still grinning at him, I think. Though panic may have set in.
I can hear the soft whine seeping from my eyes, feel my back sliding downward. I hope
for a soft thud on the linoleum. I understand this is my talent:

                                          I cannot choose the boundless freedom of wheels,
nor will I hope in the mythical land people go when they leave the children's ward.
Outside. Better. Instead, I hold on to the wall or a table or the next person, gaining
a few more moments of strength before my body forfeits its own power. Standing up
for someone like myself is an inordinate feat.

Collar Is What Hangs around the Neck

after Forrest Gander

the men in the market they knew
        me with my ambling unsteady gait knew
                nothing but the market itself and me new

I walked directly in the path
        of the sun a clear sign I was a tourist
                had a wandering about my feet weak muscles

still it was blinding like LA and like a dancing
        dizzy blur forged by heat distance inland empire
                but it was not and was Puerto Limón Costa Rica

nowhere near the white retirees
        on the Pacific Coast this was the closest east
                I had been in three months toward the Caribbean

the Jamaican men called to me
        selling their wares and I looked curiously
                back no smiling I had gotten used to settling

a line on my lips from the streets in the city
        a line against the honking cars screaming indigents passers
                by my wandering feet a sign of weakness obvious illness

I have always been sucked in
        by jewelry spying an oval necklace
                hecho por mano he says made by hand

and I Puerto Rican learned accent in tow
        give an arch *eh* point and let my tone
                bracket the word *ésta* this one

He asks to place it on me
>	I eye him using the other vendor's mirror
>	>	his tongue pokes through the side of his mouth

eyes squinting clasping the tiny sparkling buckles
>	I see him pause before he is done
>	>	feel the silver lobster claw settle at the base of my birthmark

He taps my shoulder to turn
>	I marvel at the way the ocean sits
>	>	on my skin its shimmering tans and coppers and golds

welcoming the jewel I touch my fingers
>	to the scars underneath *¿qué te hicieron?*
>	>	what have they done to you *Shit* he knows

I am american with butchered flesh
>	it's like when I was strapped in a wheelchair on the bus
>	>	and a grandfather held his toddler up *just to see*

I am a curiosity again and again *nada*
>	I answer he points to his own chest makes a line
>	>	*te entendí* I understood you he asks earnestly this time

¿pero qué pasó? es que eres tú una mujer hermosa
>	I roll my eyes startle us both with my flatness I make
>	>	my own lines my mouth my hands between us *nada*

he nods turns to show me the matching earrings
>	his own scar at his back I nod I buy both
>	>	there is a picture of me somewhere:

hands clasped in front of my mouth
>	thumbs supporting my wandering lips to a smile
>	>	necklace peeking through my wrists gaze askew

I am watching a documentary about food, again

The host thanks the baker in a halting, tremulous voice,
while the camera goes for an extreme beauty shot, neglecting

his six-foot frame. He understands how sacred
both her kitchens are, the solitude she cultivates tending them

a moment akin to hallelujah. She looks at him, explaining
her place among her people. How the food is never just food

and her body never just her own. I envy her ease
with the sweetness of it all, all the good grace.

My hands have never learned this particular art
with any degree of satisfaction. My friend tells me as much

while she paints her kitchen cabinets: *You may need to learn
how to make dessert. Everyone needs at least one recipe for something sweet.*

Of course, she says this when she believes I am dating.
But, I think about what it might mean for me alone,

to be as the baker must be: satisfied and calm in the chaos
of eggs, chocolate, raspberries, almond flour—spinning

a cake stand like a tale. I blink and he speaks my mind:
I want to taste this iteration of your freedom.

Corona Poem

The recipe lists black beans
soaked overnight in water;
I boil them in vegetable stock.

It says use white rice
because it is fluffy.
I prefer nutty brown.

Three uneven heaps
of tomato, onion, and garlic.
I don't count how much.

It doesn't mention
anything about peppers.
I slide in chilies in adobo.

Says ham hocks. Let it simmer
till meat cleaves from bone.
I chop chorizo into tiny bits. Fry it.

The directions tell me: sprinkle
cumin and oregano.
I toss in a melon baller's worth.

Cover with liquid
and bring to a boil.
I eye the pile of ingredients.

I grab what I know:
let pale golden beer slake the pot
glugging, like a dying heartbeat.

T,

On your birthday, I went to the dentist.
Ann writes that cleanings mitigate depression
so, I sat,
opened and closed.

The scaler scraping curled my fists
around the chair's handles, as if my might
could detach them for swordplay,
my triceps tight but long. You were into fencing
at least as a metaphor
thrust and parry was my ebb and flow.
I much preferred swimming.

My new hygienist informs me
one of my front teeth is out of line.
I flick it with my tongue
You can't feel it. It sounds like
she is smiling under her mask.
My debutante friends insist
people hear smiles in the voice.
Do you hear me?

During a low hum of conversation
going nowhere about shoes, books, breakfast,
the hygienist starts calling out numbers
2-3-2 on 11, 3-3-3, 2-2-3.
We want three and under. Just like that:
my maxillary incisors meet approval. Molars too.

Last time we spoke, we made plans for pancakes.
I got there and sat,
opened and closed,
before someone told me
you weren't coming.
You'd stopped eating
and it stopped you.

I make my next appointment six months to the day.

I remain,
    — me.

for Tristan H. Campbell
1983–2010

On sex

for Pauli Murray

Pauli wrote letters to the doctors, begging
for them to take a look between the legs,
or, more precisely, what lay under the skin:

Pauli thought there was more evidence
that Pauli was absolutely right, that "she" was
in fact "he," a person Pauli could understand,

and after Pauli submitted under those white sheets,
under the gown they would have discarded,
to their fingers, their knives, their eyes

(and make no mistake, this "them"
was a group of men), one of them wrote
Pauli a letter, very nicely if you can believe,

telling Pauli Pauli was mistaken about Pauli's body,
"she" was indeed female, which is to say,
the only unnatural thing about Pauli

was the thing that made them believe Pauli was male:
that very large and intimidating organ—the brain.

Palimpsestina

That's Suzanne's daughter. You know she's about your age now.
Suzanne's wedding was so glorious: Alençon lace, silk chiffon.
Where are we, honey? Am I going back to Baltimore?
Of course, I know. It's 1963. They just shot the president.
On account of my arthritis, I can't move them. These old hands.
I didn't put the kettle on. How is there water everywhere?

Did you forget you put the kettle on? It sputters everywhere.
Remember Suzanne's daughter passed. Ten years ago, now.
But you don't have arthritis. You don't know what happened to your hands?
You always said Suzanne's wedding was tacky: velveteen, polyester chiffon.
You can't go back in time just because you don't like the president.
We live in New Jersey. You don't live in Baltimore.

I love that crime show, *Law & Order*. Dun-dun. It's in Baltimore.
Cups for afternoon tea? This kitchen! Everything is everywhere!
Of course, I know. It's 1981. They just shot at the president.
I know you. You're Evan's youngest. So grown up now.
You'll want to hem that skirt. That petticoat is lightweight chiffon.
I don't want to see a doctor. Just need some aspirin for my hands.

Your fingers are bleeding. You don't know what happened to your hands?
Law & Order takes place in NY. *The Wire* is in Baltimore.
This skirt doesn't drag with heels. See? No petticoat. No chiffon.
Forty years of making afternoon tea. And, you look for cups everywhere.
Evan's youngest is Jill. That's Sophie. About six now.
You can't go back in time just because you don't like the president.

Of course, I know. It's 1994. They just shot at the president.
I don't know what happened last night. A pot crushed my hands?
My husband should be back from the grocer any minute now.
Billie Holiday is from here. She sang "Strange Fruit." Storms come out of Baltimore.
I need to make myself some tea. Things feel off, everywhere.
You'll be a beautiful bride. No mermaid mess. Just A-line, Chantilly lace, chiffon.

I've already gotten married. My dress had tulle. Mom, I hate chiffon.
You can't go back in time just because you don't like the president.
Some tea would be good. My mind is nowhere and everywhere.
Can you tell me where you were last night when the pot fell on your hands?
Yes, Billie Holiday. Frederick Douglass. "The Star Spangled Banner." All Baltimore.
That's right. Daddy said he wanted to get ice cream. Back any minute now.

All this about chiffon sharpens the limit of a single pair of hands.
What to do about presidents who could give a fuck about Baltimore?
And we are thinking every where, every why is a "What now?"

The Amateur Gardener Contemplates Trauma

Little pamphlets say: *Be careful! The garden will be overrun.* One day, there are nine. The next: twenty-seven. The grape tomatoes drag their stems lower now to the ground. The roots rip, the caked brown of the dirt like dried blood. Roots are sinews of exposed muscle that still reach for nourishing ground; their naked nodules, gaping sores. I do what I can, watering them daily. Scooping more dirt. Letting the bushy cherry tomato plant grow sideways as it needs, though I help stabilize its smaller cousin. The small yellow flowers eventually do turn green, their fruit a bright, stopping color. My constant presence reassures the plant and the pests.

                         embittered strange fruit
                         pick only the ready ones
                         taste and see what's good

Apostrophe to Inspiration

Look, bitch, I done told you
we not friends no more.
You kept telling me that
I was the best you ever seen
the best you ever had
and I believed you.

I wanted to believe you so bad.

That's the thing about sparkling baubles;
they go with everything.
I'm about to Coco Chanel this motherfucker.

Because remember:
when you kept insisting
I was one of your children,
you coddled me under a wing,
fed me from your own mouth:
let me feast on my having been,
I mean, my being
a beacon, a lighthouse for all wrecked
by common human concerns.

I am the open door in the distance,
welcoming the perfectionist.
I am the one
standing, yes standing
at a formidable height, say 5'11",
with slender build and cocoa skin.

I am the one people look to
when they whisper, *I can do it*.
But, girl, you lied.

You didn't tell me
that version of myself was a mirage.
They see it for real; it's their choice.
They thirst for a reality that dries
in the scorching of a daily existence.

Ordinary people are poets, true,
but ordinariness is not the province of poets.
Between the wash, meals, work, caretaking—
we all need a little of you.
But you sell us a wish,
hope with feathers unattached to anything.

I'm not willing to be that vision anymore.
I am as I am: sometimes
seated, yes seated
in my chair, my gnarled feet, my exploding
waistline. I am real. I am not a shining light
or maybe I am

just brighter because of everything else.

Chronically Ill

"Mothafucka, I'm ill. Not sick." —Lil Wayne, "A Milli"

You can't get away from the bodies. They drop
like a beat, all that velocity, all that heart.

Mean and vicious like an IV snaking its way
up your arm or a tube down your throat.

Hip-hop like pissing off nurses and doctors,
making friends with orderlies & food servers.

You can't stop this hustle: don't make enough
for SSI to take your check. Don't make enough

to blow up that good thing you got going
with that connect over in durable medical supplies.

I actually crip walk. Y'all just swaggerjack
off the old heads with polio and cerebral palsy.

Who you got on your squad? We got next.
Prodigy. Ms. Lauryn Hill. Fetty Wap. T-Boz on the hook.

Possibly Kanye but we don't really want him either.
Here's the thing: we been out here paper chasing

on some basic necessity type shit: food, clothing, shelter.
But we got time to make music, make the shit you groove to,

so, if you gon' take our names, go all the way,
take the blood and the screams. Do nothing by halves.

We are nothing if not whole.

On recompense

$3,120. That's how much Congress gave
Harriet Tubman for back pay.
In 1898, she demanded, yes, demanded
that they compensate her labor:
nurse, cook, commander, all-around
badass. (Though I am certain
that last one was subject to omission.)
Dancing to the tune of surprise,
they must have fixed their eyebrows
like wings, mumbling about fairness.

After all, she slew the dragons at Combahee,
forged the path from the lost, left
behind a husband, and more. Besides,
hadn't she been kicked in the head?
Didn't she dream dreams?
She spoke with the fluency
of freedom: that is, to their ears,
money, and to mine, pride.

They say that's about $100,000
in today's money. Truth is,
trying to imagine her world
is like looking through mesh wire screens:
the color rimmed by an impossible darkness.
You can't unsee it.
You don't want to.

I tell her some of her ancestors must have snitched on Harriet Tubman,

and I see her face go slack, how she's acting right now settles over her eyes. She looks at me needing her blackity black ass support on today. The day is longer than usual. No, literally; the sun hangs out in the sky as if it too knows the beat down happens after school, but before the street lights come on. Her grandmother grabs her by her shoulder so hard her tears catch the wind before she can say anything. Her stuttering voice tries to convince her nana nothing happened. That lie makes its way back: her nana calls up that school so that every teacher knows that no one can hurt her baby. Of course, her nana thinks it was a teacher. Of course, her nana doesn't know it was her own damn fault. Here Mrs. Schlepter comes asking me what all had happened. I raise my eyebrows so they look like wings. I hold out my hands, palms up, say what my mother tells me instead of *That's none of your business.* The tension did ease out my chest that night. I brushed my teeth thinking about when my brother threw down with Maximus up the street for calling him Maxi-mouse and I told my brother that boy's daddy named him after a gladiator because he wanted him to be strong. When his daddy died like ours, that name was all they had left except for funeral money. I tried to understand why she didn't stick up for me. Trying to imagine her world was like looking through mesh wire screens. As soon as it gets clear, all you see are rows of squares. I knew I wasn't wrong but she wasn't right neither. And standing there alone was the hardest and best thing I think I had ever done up until that point. Maybe walking away was the hardest thing she ever done.

What You Don't See When Ben Vereen Guest Stars as Will's Father on *The Fresh Prince,* May 1994

What everyone talks about is that final scene: Lou/Ben Vereen walks out and Will screams and Uncle Phil/James Avery hugs Will. This is that hard emoting no one really likes to see in a sitcom since, apparently, "very special episodes" disappeared after the 1980s.

What everyone forgets about is that this aired after Mother's Day. An arc when Will thinks about fathers. John Witherspoon cannot coordinate as Will's girlfriend's eccentric pilot father. Will's best friend, Jazz, wants to be a daddy. Jazz's wife wants Will to be her baby daddy. Carlton is Carlton.

What everyone sees is that Will jitters around Lou. All of a sudden, his shirt collar is awry. Adjust that. His mouth turns down. Adjust that. The Fresh Prince now has an unmistakable stutter in the lingua franca of not-committed. Just that.

I heard that Will improvises his final lines. Uncle Phil—who never is anything but mirth and frustration—now has a trembling silence that will not stay on B-roll. That is Karyn Parsons's sob punctuating the final credits.

What everybody glides over is that Lou reaches for basketball, as though that's the only language Will knows even though Will gets served on the court in the opening credits, because it is the only way Lou can follow through; and, when Will looks at his younger self perched on another Black man's shoulders—*Swoosh!*—he thinks he's finally got that smooth lay-up kind of father, the kind of father that little boy grows up to have when he plays Myles on *Moesha* since Myles will know Black father love for six seasons.

What y'all don't know is that James Avery and Ben Vereen need a hand clap. They are trained theater actors, framed by an impossibly buoyant gray couch, ottoman, one and a half chair, majestic spiral staircase, French doors, vestibule off stage right, chef's kitchen stage left, and a live studio audience. They give you unvarnished growl and gesticulation, soliloquy in the key of Negro major, smooth disappointment and cool resentment rivalling the afterlives of Caliban and Shylock.

What had happened was in 1981 Ben Vereen performed in blackface at Reagan's inaugural. None of us ever forgot it. Not the Black. Not the face. Not none of it. The whole Black world been wanted Lou to not be Ben for a minute, someone who couldn't walk out on Will after twenty-two minutes, not after fifteen sitcom years, not after thirteen real-life years neither.

MIND YOU

What Had Happened Was

What had happened was I learned to love me later on:
when no one was looking, I massaged a callus
mistaking it for muscle, cascading pressure,
alternating misrecognition. Clutching, sometimes rolling—
the pad of my finger circled the edges of contusions,
until I began to tell myself an unvarnished story:
I hate me (present tense). Oh! You thought
this was a story about redemption. Could be. Could be not.

These days, I am doing what my therapist calls
sitting with it. I do not enjoy this. I am become one
in need. Contrary to how I prefer to understand myself,
as a steady, constant force—air, water, fire—
changing as much as mood. As with any now,
I don't know, which is to say, I don't want to.

I say, "I don't want to know" rather than say,
my classroom was the roughest you could not imagine:
four white walls, a landscape watercolor, and the constant
shrill chirp of machines. A cadre of new faces each day
shouting, yammering at me after much sleeplessness.
In they would march, papers at hand, rating on a scale
of not really to never, how good my body could be.
I had never failed at anything, even defending myself.
This was a considerably top-notch success then: autoimmune
illness that affects, as the statistics said, only three
out of twenty-five thousand. As with most tests, I ranked
in the smallest percentile. Twelve years old felt like
an awfully long life at the time. I waited to die. I waited
forever to learn simple things—love, heart, song.

These things—love, heart, song—take forever to learn.
And of all the songs to sing, the ones from the heart,
who sings a Black girl's song? Who sings in the hitching
tune of this Black girl's body?

I took a knife to my skin, one day, knowing I needed
to slice parallel to the arm but I had nothing
to numb the possibility of pain:
so, I put the knife to other uses. Gliding

my tongue across my teeth, fingernails across the page,
in a rocking motion. A chef says, *Go for accuracy,
the speed will come*. I am always four fingers down,
thumb curved in, chopping it up, becoming someone new,

keeping the sound thick like layered vocals. Remembering how
I flayed my skin so it could sizzle on a rock defying the sun.

Yes, I flayed my skin so it could sun itself on a rock.
This, of course, is painful. Torture, one might say. Murder. Ritual.

Not quite unlike lighting candles or self-immolation on the flame.
On an ordinary day, I called this friendship, patiently—

from the Latin root *patior* meaning "to suffer"—waiting
for a returned phone call, an invitation, the crossing of a mind.

Years like this, desiccating, staring out of hospital windows,
breathing coerced by science. It is a specific kind of misery—

as in the Old French *miserie*, that is "wretched."
I quite enjoy the allusion to an elderly woman,

if only because my illness usually only affects the geriatric,
and I have experienced the coldness of being forgotten:

meaning I opened up the thickest part to scrutiny. I recuperated:
soaking my feet in pineapple water, cloves, and cinnamon.

I soaked my feet in pineapple water, cloves, and cinnamon
because I thought it would relieve my pain
because I thought the feet were a road map to the whole body
because if my feet were clean my whole self was also
because they said so
because it made sense at the time
because I read somewhere that plants could cure me
because what else is there left but this detoxifying
and all of my relationships would benefit from this sweet
and spicy combination I stirred the pot
because I heard the siren call of the past
because I needed a role model mentor expert hand
because a bird whistled the day the sky turned crisp yellow
because I heard it would make you beautiful

And what if it did not make me beautiful?
What then?

As when encountering a stair and realizing I was not
strong enough to scale it. I mean that literally.

As when being asked to smile and I could not
part my lips in the half moon that creates warmth.

That too I mean literally. I was everything they told me
to be: passive bodied, vulnerable, in need of rescue.

A woman with a disability is the perfect archetype
of woman. She can let men have, do, be.

But there is the simple matter of color within those lines—
a loud and unyielding shade. I did make a valiant effort

to make a something of myself, a recognizable something:
a sketch, a portrait of grace. That is all I ever wanted.

That was all I ever wanted: for the pen to sketch a portrait,
like those in history, those displayed with lights overhead, hung
in galleries. What photographers would call a medium shot, cut off
at the knees, commanding gaze, sitting to indicate leisure, stretched
over the canvas in colors designed to withstand all historical wear
and permanence.

I know about Mary Turner, the woman they said
enraged the mob with her words, how she was burned, her child
sliced from her womb, crushed under bootheel. This is the opaque history
into which I've slipped: one where I speak despite
the erasure, the consequence.

I am not so far from Mrs. Turner. I think in terms of the time.
I think in terms of the body. The remainder after divide and conquer,
left of the centerpiece, the master's piece. The showstopper.

When I am the centerpiece, the masterpiece, the showstopper,
I don't know what to do. I sit in the way of all queens:
stiff, smiling, waving, and, a little bored.

I know what I have done to become this. Truly, I was good:
I behaved and did as I was told. I followed all the rules.
It is a lonely place; this private section of firsts and wheelchairs only.

At the Seattle Aquarium, the staff let me touch a sea urchin.
They selected one accustomed to humanity, a good one, they said.
I stroked its flesh. The pads of my finger were, they said, harmless.

It was alive, moving even, but not reactive. Tired, I rued.
I withdrew my finger from the tank with a tenderness
I only now understand as a poem. I have the photo, evidence

that I was once part of the scene rather than prey
to flashing lights, burning my eyes to possess the soul inside them.

I'll admit I let my soul burn out, the eyes flashing from inside,
but I am wending my way back. Over surgeries, and hospital
stays, isolation. Over medications, appointments. Over my dead body.

That's right. You can die from this. Plainly put:
the treatments cost. I have to make it rain every month
at the physician's office. I also pay in time.

Opportunity cost benefit analysis. That is, food, meds, or independence.
It is that simple.   It is that complicated.
And, of course, how to secure a job when you need accommodating?

If this pandemic taught me anything, it was that a doctor could kill me
because I am out of time: a body with no future, and too much past.
And, the internet is internetting, telling me to find my joy

in the simplest of pleasures. My energy should be like a whispering lover:
"What do you dream in summer?"

Do you dream of cherries?
Rainier. Chelan. Montmorency. English Morello in jars.
I confess. I like the regular ones: Bing. That lovely exhale
of air before the vowel silences itself inside your mouth,
just where you taste its sweetness, on the soft palate.
Yes, like that. Bing.

Beginning in May, I pierce the red flesh, leaving bite marks
that revel in the nudity of a seed. Sometimes I do not spit,
sometimes I enjoy working my tongue over the wetness,
leaving a core cleaved from its home. What I'm saying is this:

I enjoy these details in the heat, at least, in this part of my body.
It offers something delightful, in exchange for small labors,
provided I do not abandon it, savor via refusal.
Can you imagine this joy so slow it aches like a pulse?

I do. I mean, I have tried to.
Here, too, I like what is regular, a constant traffic
of love from me to, well, me.
On days I barely had the strength to stand,
when my legs felt like water, I opened myself only
to the beautiful padded walls of a book—
the thickness of newly pressed pages, crisp serifs
and the curves of plotline—where I left myself behind.
I was living in the regency era. HIV/AIDS epidemic
Los Angeles. Yesterday. I forgot myself
inside the spaces between the words, the characters'
small quirks. I became who I always wanted to be.
Someone else. Do you understand this disconnect?
Actually, I think I'm asking, am I on time?

Actually, I think I'm asking, are you on time?
Because I know I am not. That is, I have an issue
with chronology. It is called a chronic illness:
that is, it occurs and recurs, a river running over
the same rock each day, wearing a groove:
rather, according to a clock, and a calendar,
I have none of the time in the world, at least,
it doesn't belong to me.
This is the story of the feeble. And, of deity. Who decides
the tick tick boom of whether I walk or fall,
blink or smile? The muscles have a mind of their own.
Each day, they have their own schedule.
That is a reckoning. This, too, seems divine.
Chronos, what do you mean? O, father of chaos and the ether.

Chronos, yes, the father of Chaos and Ether:
They say he produced all the other deities,
and, like all fathers, represents a cycle
of disappointments. Oh, well, that's not fair.
Not all fathers.
Anyway, I suspect that his lover got tired
of the recurring problems, more spiral than circle,
drifting toward a kind of slow inevitable void.
As the story goes, this is why all narrative is a mirror
of male orgasm. That feels petty. And, yet, true.
But my story, my entanglement with chronos, ends differently.
A conversion tale, a cautionary tale: if you like,
kairos, or being brought to life.

After all, *kairos* breathes stories, whispers inconveniently
like when you have to pee at the best part of the film,
or silence found in traffic, that midsentence finger pausing
on a page of otherwise unremarkable prose.

That's the thing. You never can tell when time will stop,
open up its starving maw for you to clamber through.
You never can tell because it is just so fucking random
how that blank space opens up:

(

)

I mean... So tell me why... It went like this...
Aight, so, boom. What had happened was...

What had happened was I learned to love me later on
which is to say, I don't know or even want to say why
these things—love, heart, song—take forever to learn.

I flayed my skin so it could sizzle on a rock defying the sun.
I soaked my feet in pineapple water, cloves, and cinnamon
because I heard it would make me beautiful.

That is all I ever wanted: to be the subject of a portrait
as the centerpiece, I mean, the masterpiece, the showstopper—
flashing lights illuminate the eyes, possess the soul inside them.

Tell me something: do you dream of cherries in summer?
I do. I mean, I have tried to.
Actually, I think I'm asking, are we on time?

Chronos, what you mean, is the father of chaos and the ether,
while Kairos, what I mean, requires me to bring it to life.

& THE THIRD

Variation on a Theme

after Gwendolyn Brooks and other furious flowers

We tired, two syllables, no are. We
real tired cuz we tried to listen for real for real.
Cool. Not for play play. We kept our cool.

We keep tryin to save ourselves. We
left our own selves behind in case things went left.
School must reopen, they say. We can't reopen school.

We keep other folks and other things in mind. We
lurk in our homes and behind masks, lurk
late at night in our trembling thoughts. Lately,

we think about all the kinds of work we do.
Strikes seem a good idea. Back in the day, striking
straightened up a company, so here's some straight talk.

We tellin you: we feel this apocalypse in our bones. We
sing to thee of Shine and his hustle. We be singin
sinfully, all them low notes about keeping a piece, since

we know ain't nobody thinking about us. We:
thin boned and called essential. A lie so thin
genuine care slips through plus vermouth, lemon, bitters, gin.

We toast the inevitable cuz we know. We
jazz up the coming breathlessness. We listen for March jazz
in June. We been in the house since March. It's June.

We know there may not be an end. For if we must
die, we choose which monster murders us. Some of us will die
soon.

Potential Ode or Elegy Out My Window

Yesterday, there were two people walking: a young Black one
in sweats and a black coat splayed against the wind
(walking with purpose and rhythm I don't often see up here in Maine),
locs in a half ponytail, edges shaped and the Timbs looked like
they were spit shined,
looked like someone cared;
the older white one,
in sweats and a black coat splayed against the wind,
walked on the same sidewalk, hobbling so as to not fall,
tripped up by stubborn tree roots & the city
refusing to repair sidewalks, walking too with purpose, green mittens
grabbing at whatever could steady a gait.

Sometimes, I take to watching my window
like television: the schoolchildren
who enter & escape the middle school,
the crowds for sporting events
at the old armory, the semiannual gun show
when I black out my windows and pretend I'm not home,
Halloween,
when I black out my windows and pretend I'm not home.

The young Black person came behind,
veered into the street
so as to not overtake
passed near the gutter
so as to not be overtaken,
then stepped onto the sidewalk somewhere near
my front door, beyond my view.
The white person only noticed belatedly and
kept walking, only to pause at my neighbor's
peeling brown siding, goldenrod trim, and faded American flag
an unpaired parenthesis splayed against the wind.

Neighborhood Watch

after Ilya Kaminsky

Mrs. Vandersotten, 48, might actually have a third eye
one for what Stevie Wonder called inner visions
and perhaps also a fourth
that lets her know when neighborhood kids behave like hooligans.

She sits in her front garden
encased by a fence.
All we see is her bobbing head over each picket.
We think she talks to the flowers
between resolving our disputes.

Mrs. Vandersotten, Kam said Pluto is a planet. Is Pluto a planet?
On a good day, she'd answer.
On a better day, she'd say, *Look it up.*
Mrs. Vandersotten, who's faster: me or Kam?
I wasn't watching. She'd lie. *Run down the street again.*
We'd run. She'd say, *My husband. Fastest thing on two legs.*
He hightailed it out of here and never came back.
We looked at each other having never got that detail before.

We started to ask other adults questions
about her while we waited
to get too old to play outside.
Like how did a Black woman get a Dutch name?
And, where did her husband go anyway? And, why?
My mother told me stay out of grown folks' business.
Kam's brother said he cheated and she kicked him out.
Kam asked if that was the case why was his dad still around?
Kam's brother said stay out of grown folks' business.

Last summer, Kam and me got into a fight.
I pushed against his bird chest. He mine.
Mrs. Vandersotten called, *Young men!*
We stopped. Kam asked, *Well, Mrs. Vandersotten,*
who you think the strongest?
And, she said, *Ya mama.*

Coming Home

I tap on our door with one
knuckle, let swinging suitcases
careen on the downbeat, arc
between my gentler digit and silence.

It is all too heavy to set down,
too heavy to carry.
You've wait up for me. You don't
let this beat linger a beat longer.

You take both suitcases and unfull
my hands. The coat, too. *Thank you.*
The shoes slip off. Your head brushes
my cheek. A vibrato breath. Mm.

I rush to unhook my bra, come
up out this gear. You pause, before asking,
How was your trip? The tea is waiting;
my drink is waiting for me.

You blink, rub your eyes,
the odd restlessness of sleeping alone,
how you reached out, found cool cotton.
Your smile creeps from the center of your mouth.

You are a wall of a man, a broad door.
I lean to, let idle prattle fall between us,
drinks warming our hands. We laugh,
the weight lifting from my voice.

The events are too heavy to set down;
they are too heavy to carry.
You take my cup toward the sink,
the pile of mugs, the mocha rings inside.

You once joked: you only brew coffee
when you miss me, a rich ginger hot roast,
pleasant earth to sink into and I arch
an eyebrow knowing

how it glides on your tongue,
warming that soft palate under the nose.
My thumb coaxes the wet from your upper lip.
Kiss the me on you.

This is the door.
This is the door and you let me in.

Ranunculus

so im sitting in annamarias house right in her living room right so like shes got this gorg wooden table like oak cedar or something and on it is this candle and im like whoa a candle but just sos you dont think im crazy its like nearly down to its little emerald nub but like just enough for dinner and in this killer little glass holder that looks like its got a better figure than me like for real and next to it like right next to it is a bottle with three flowers but like the bottle was old school liquor like hard liquor bottle with one of those crow masks on it like the ones you see in sex dungeons i mean not that ive ever been to a sex dungeon or whatever but like ive got hbo so anyway three flowers in there one white with like rose tips the flower totally has a french mani situation and then behind it is this little pink number that looks like a tutu but in the center so like thats the one that kills me because it is such a little star in this fresh little liquor bottle turned vase or is it vase whatever so theres this fuschia flower the color of that little number i like to wear in august just enough red and just enough sex and it is totally setting off the olive in the curtains all that matte in the candle the light is looking so pretty outside as it goes down but back to this flower its a peony no thats not it a ranunculus really sounds like a disease and the petals are interlaid like shingles on a roof the ranunculus is just clutching them so tight and all i can think to ask the flower is please tell me little ranunculus tell me all of your pretty secrets

It was just before Thanksgiving

The day my mother left my father for good, my cousin came to fetch me from school.

I was in the third row with my rolled-tight bangs and dent from pink sponge curlers.

I was dropping in midmorning fatigue. I cannot remember exactly what I wore.

I just picture my fifth-grade photo: red Sally Jesse Raphael glasses, a multicolored sweater.

It had blue and pink stripes with a constellation of silver sparkles in my chest galaxy.

My mother stuffed clothing into a Pony gym bag. I grabbed books and Danny Doggy.

I wanted to get my red crayon bank but, because my brother stole, there was nothing in it.

We left behind that tiny kitchen where I lay on the counter to get my hair washed.

There was a small refrigerator with my $50 savings bond on top from my first piece of writing.

The front room was where we danced to Michael Jackson's *Thriller*, stomping.

Mrs. Tate, the downstairs landlord, banged on the ceiling with her broom.

I left behind my big room with its tea set and stuffed animals arranged for playing school.

In the green bathroom, Grandma used to run my wrists under cold water to stop my nosebleeds.

I think my sheets were yellow.

We ate drive-thru, drove into the pharmaceutical sunset, and raced double yellow lines.

I will tell my mother I barely remember the story and I do or I don't, so I write hers.

June 2018

there is a picture of my mother
 white shirt & Adidas track pants
 her hair slightly undone
  smiling as she rubs her pregnant belly

   in her white tee & track pants
    her hand moving over belly over hand
     smiling as she rubs her pregnant belly
      I will not tumble out the way I am supposed to

       refusing her hand over belly over hand
        I have to be cut out
         I will not tumble out the way I am supposed to
          stolen from the only home I knew

           I have cut out
            this process will repeat years later
             stolen from the only home I know
              I am rubbing my own belly

               this process repeats later this year
                hand over belly over hand
                 I am rubbing my own belly
                  I cannot believe what is under

                   hand over belly over hand
                    white shirt & track pants
                     I cannot believe what is under
                      this growing strangeness inside

                   in my white tee & Adidas track pants
                    what will not come tumbling out as it is supposed to
                     this growing strangeness inside
                      my body has to be cut

              what will not come tumbling out as it is supposed to
               hand over belly over hand
                my body has to be cut
this is a picture of my mother

Ursa Corregidora Goes to Junior High in the 1990s

I'm in the principal office for giving this boy a knuckle tap to the temple & his mama there and my mama ain't. The principal ask what happened, say ladies first. Smile. So I say I was wearing my gym shorts & minding my own business & he say that ain't what happen. I cross my arms til principal say go on. So I tell them about how he shoulda never been looking at my behind cuz ain't nothing there for him. & how even if he just happen to see something he don't know me like that to go picking it off. & how come if he so innocent then why was him & them other boys laughing, huh? & his mama look away, wrinkle her nose. The boy say he just was being nice & I wanted him to touch me. I say Naw. His mama narrow her eyes a little bit. & the principal ask where my mama at? & I shrug, don't say nothing 'bout how some people literally don't have no time for this shit. The two of them look at me like I shoulda never been wearing the shorts no how. & I think they all I got. I look at his mama looking at me, saying nothing. & I wonder whether she making a generation of boys like this here principal. & the principal ask why come my shorts so short. His mama say that ain't the question here. She grab the boy ear & twist it, whisper all up in his skull. He say:
I didn't mean it.
I ain't raised to be no boy that hurt people.
I say I don't want no boys hurting me.
He say I don't wanna be a boy that hurt people.
I say don't hurt me.

Some Suicides Are Slow

Skip medications,
forget which ones
mix well.
Does pink oblong gel
and round scored
tangerine go
with food or before
breakfast?
Forget meals
and showers,
let the mold grow
in skin folds
over the thigh,
or at the back,
cascading
like shoals
at the shore
of a spine.
Don't buy
a remedy,
eat
the sugar,
the salt,
the white bread
all together:
one glorious
PBJ
and a pickle.
Order
in but tip
real good.
Gobble
with no water—

avian pecking,
darting the neck
down, and sideways.
Choose to lay
down, refuse
to walk, and fire
the trainer. This
is a working
woman's slow careen.
Rather, an extinguishing
desire
for slumber. More.

I got into a Twitter beef with Lolo Jones over a blind white girl

the blind girl lands a shot put where it's supposed to land & the crowd is amazed at the amazingly talented girl who throws shot puts while blind. the amazing blind shot putter & i roll my eyes & i roll them so hard my fingers spit out words & lolo jones says she's not getting pity claps lolo says this isn't because she's blind i say to myself u were supposed to be a hero & u were supposed to be a competitor who understood what it is to be different but i've got too much home training to say she's just a bootleg flo jo so i write all intelligently & put that phd stank on the tweet the claps are by definition pity. people would not be clapping if they could have seen what she saw which is that she didn't need eyes to land the shot put & i'm so mad i log off & i unfollow & i block her ass too & years later when i see allyson felix's scar i think allyson might have understood what had happened she woulda got it. the difference between changing your mind & confirming it 'cause she's black like lolo black like me but i'm more like that white girl with my body that people think is a whole lot of can't & i wish i would see lolo on the street one day & i just know she gonna recognize me & be like we got beef & i swear imma be like lolo imma vegetarian

What Cliff Should Have Told Theo on the Pilot of *The Cosby Show*, September 1984

In the pilot, there was no Princeton-going Sondra,
the eldest Huxtable kid, who would've been in the same cohort as Michelle,
but there was no screen time available for Black misfits
neither from Chicago nor Brooklyn. (& Sondra never
brought home friends. Only that sad-ass Elvin.)

Theo's desire to be "regular people" would later be called self-actualization
but would never be called by its proper name except in Black circles.

Vanessa's dour character would never improve
in eight seasons, nor would her hair.

When Theo is calculating his monthly income,
he does not factor in whether he will get paid biweekly,
how many busted rubbers result in paternity, and stop
& frisk. There will also be an emotional cost
to realizing you've squandered what wealth
fictional Black parents built. Against the odds still.

Even in the language of Quaaludes no won't never not be no.

Clair's career is not on-screen. She only exists
in the kitchen and the bedroom, so her being
an attorney is not apparent.
Only Theo's mouth takes her outside home.

"I brought you in this world / and I can take you out"
was supposed to give Cliff a moment of unobtrusive Reagan-era Blackness.
Clair muttering on the stairs in English and Spanish
was supposed to give her a moment of unobtrusive Reagan-era Blackness.

Denise's first date with the merchant marine gave Lisa Bonet
the wanderlust needed for her sudden departure from the port
of Brooklyn to a different world and finally her mooring
in the deeply conservative embraces of Joseph C. Phillips and Raven-Symoné.

By the time Theo grew up, they would have gentrified New Jersey.

$200 for having a girlfriend would never have been enough.

Antony and Cleopatra, dir. Simon Godwin, National Theatre, 2019

The speaker gives us the history
we well know about Antony and Cleopatra:

the petulant ruler redux & she who was queen,
the Shakespearean interpretation of their love.

Cleopatra cannot be desired
how she wishes; Antony cannot love
anyone but himself & his own power.

The speaker points to the screen. Two actors
almost kissing but not, talking too closely but not.

This Cleopatra, her head in a crown of braids, stares
straight at this Antony, with balding pate, scarce red hairs

wrinkles above his brow. She looks
on the verge of telling the big secret,
the one that kills him in the end:

what she wills with her brown skin, glistening in the still,
listening to him drone, and whispering his name.

The speaker says Antony needs to embrace
his own melancholy to love Cleopatra well.

I hear Antony does not want this
blues kind of love. Antony does not want
this blues. Antony does not

want to want. I see Cleopatra's braids unravel, she slides
across the divan as she rises to miss his kiss:

the silk tatters at her feet, the feet posed for speech,
the speech in her hands. We know what comes next.

But, this is a still with the not-kissing, the fabric undulating
at her ankle, hems sharp as the truth on her lips,
fingers tense enough to handle snakes.

my lover says

he doesn't remember the first time he touched me with purpose,
not his callused hands running the arc of my bicep flush warm
from the summerized city, or even the wet hot air courtesy of urban
heat indices, not my body lit by stars nestled in a billowing gray dark,
in the cool of his shadow, hair covering my closed-eye wakefulness.
After all these years, I don't recall why
I remember what I do except that it all feels necessary to keep
close, some secret in his fingertips with their buzz raising the soft hairs,
my willing waist waiting, wilting into the cushion under the hum
of his gaze, close like my legs and lips pressed together, in tense
preparation for the grasp that breaks my odalisque repose, the mark
of us awakening to who we were to each other.

I meet a man with a stutter

and I cannot stop gazing at his mouth
the way the full lips shape the air,
the quiver of flesh at nothingness.
He has something they call a block stutter
meaning he pauses between words
and the golden brown of his cheeks vibrates
with air. Eyebrows raised, forehead creased—
a set of waved lines against his impossibly straight
hairline—he widens his walnut-shaped eyes.
I swear he winks at me. I cannot stop looking.
His voice, its fluency, in other words,
sounds like the saxophone he later plays.
I'm not particularly adept at the details of music,
but I hear something that makes my own mouth
gape open. I swear it was something about birds.
Let me be a ruby-throated hummingbird,
settling inside the silent spaces for nectar;
let me be a scarlet-throated tanager,
finding her home in the places other women abandoned;
or, perhaps your red-throated loon,
the pair of us with voices haunting the skies.
I murmur assent, less breath than sound,
realizing he hasn't yet said anything
about a girlfriend. I cannot stop staring,
which actually means I am asking questions
of his body, of my body actually. Inquisitive behind
my glasses. I push them further up the bridge
of my nose, brazen in using my left ring finger.
I swear I cannot stop myself from admiring
his mouth, which is now not moving,
his eyes, which are now rapidly blinking,
since it is my turn to say something.

Let Me Holla at You Right Quick; or Notes

I am grateful to the publications that took a chance on me and provided a home for my work: "*On March 12, 2020, Breonna Taylor*," *Langston Hughes Review*; "*Antony and Cleopatra*, dir. Simon Godwin, National Theatre, 2019" and "Variation on a Theme," *Prairie Schooner*; "Customary Calculus for Chronicity," *The Ending Hasn't Happened Yet* and *Omnium Gatherum Quarterly*; "On Losing; A Hypothesis" and "*It was just before Thanksgiving*," *Omnium Gatherum Quarterly*; "Ursa Corregidora Goes to Junior High in the 1990s," *The Journal* (Pushcart Prize nominee).

Thank you to the people who saw potential in the early versions of this manuscript: an earlier version of the manuscript was a semifinalist for the 2022 Elixir Press Poetry Award and the 2022 Lexi Rudnitsky First Book Prize. It was a finalist for the 2020 Bergman Prize from Changes Press, 2020 Hudson Prize from Black Lawrence Press, and 2022 National Poetry Series.

The four epigraphs that frame this collection form the basis of much of my storytelling as a poet and scholar. Barbara Christian as a thinker has consistently been a voice for trusting the creativity and ingenuity of my (and everyone else's) everyday Blacknesses. At first, I wanted to use the more well-known quotation about people of color theorizing in the everyday, but it struck me that this collection relies on, courts, and embraces the unruliness of variety, multiplicity, and eroticism. What's more, Christian describes how freeing the multihyphenate creative experience can be. Her words, in some fundamental ways, explained me to myself: I feel freest when I inhabit my writing as both poet and scholar, theorist and pragmatist, strategist and conduit.

Christian's work calls to each poem in the way that Octavia E. Butler does because, after all, what good is literature—in this case, poetry—for Black people? Butler's sarcasm in "Positive Obsession" scolds readers who question her decision to write as her imagination dictates. I appreciate her defiance even more after having spent time with the evidence of her mind, the archive at the Huntington Library, Art Museum, and Botanical Gardens. Butler followed her imagination, insisted on play, and embraced complexity: in so doing, she left the gate open. I've walked right on in.

One of my contemporaries (and writerly role models), Eve L. Ewing, startled me in the best way possible when I read her book *1919*. She found the possibility of poetry in the archive and pulled it out. I read her scholarly monograph, *Ghosts in the Schoolyard*, alongside the poetry collection *1919*: they are siblings intellectually. Most fascinating to me is her unflinching I/eye, the refusal to ignore the disturbing realities of white supremacy and how the past sits next to us, or meets us at the grocery store. "I saw Emmett Till this week at the grocery store" haunts me, as does the rhythm of "Jump / Rope." Her abecedarian "Coming from the Stock Yards" asks compelling questions of form (what if the rhythm of prayer explained the rupture of human connection?), of memory (what if the mnemonic device of the alphabet led us to a space of both promise and pain?), and of speech (what if someone tried to say the quiet part out loud?). Her methodology of "what if" upturned the phrase and the activity as being one largely of anxiety to being one of future-scaping and imagination.

Lil' Kim's verse on "Quiet Storm (Remix)" with Mobb Deep begins with a femmage: MC Lyte's "10% Dis" letting us know that she is coming after those who kept saying that she didn't write her own rhymes. Couched as it is in bravado and braggadocio, the message is clear: I am in a lineage of Black women rappers/writers making their mark, cementing her status as a leader. While I have no such intellectual or personal beefs, Kim's insistent confidence speaks to the conceit of writing poetry, in whatever form. Particularly from a writer steeped in hip-hop as a lingua franca, the sanctity of artistry, the love of the form, and the exhilaration of it all makes the real shit, shit to make you feel shit.

I am grateful for the following permissions:

> Excerpt from Barbara Christian's "The Race for Theory." This quotation originated from the article in *Cultural Critique*, no. 6, "The Nature and Context of Minority Discourse" (Spring 1987): 51–63. Permission granted from University of Minnesota Press and Najuma Henderson.

Octavia E. Butler, excerpt from "Positive Obsession," from *Bloodchild* and Other Stories. First published as "Birth of a Writer" in *Essence*, May 1989. Copyright © 1989, 1996, 2005 by Octavia E. Butler. Reprinted with the permission of The Permissions Company, LLC, on behalf of Seven Stories Press, sevenstories.com.

Excerpt from Eve L. Ewing's *1919* (Haymarket, 2019). Permission granted by the author.

"QUIET STORM (Remix)" by Albert J. Johnson, Kejuan Waliek Muchita, Melvin Glover, and Sylvia Robinson. © Sugar Hill Music Publishing (BMI). All Rights Administered by Warner Chappell Music Canada Ltd. All Rights Reserved. Used by Permission of Alfred Music.

"Quiet Storm (Remix)." Words and Music by Kejuan Muchita, Albert Johnson, Melvin Glover, Sylvia Robinson, and Kimberly Jones. Copyright © 1999 by Universal Music—MGB Songs, Juvenile Hell, Universal Music—Careers, P. Noid Publishing, Liquid Liquid Publishing, and Kimberly Jones Publishing Designee. All Rights for Juvenile Hell and Liquid Liquid Publishing Administered by Universal Music—MGB Songs. All Rights for P. Noid Publishing Administered by Universal Music—Careers. International Copyright Secured All Rights Reserved. Reprinted by Permission of Hal Leonard LLC.

On March 12, 2020, Breonna Taylor

This poem would not be possible without the reporting of the *New York Times* podcast *The Daily* in its two-part series "The Killing of Breonna Taylor," September 9 and 10, 2020, hosted by Michael Barbaro.

Getting Dressed

When I was consulting with the Metropolitan Museum of Art's "Crip the Met" initiative, Ian Alteveer told us the story about Camille Pissarro on our tour of the museum. It struck me that Pissarro was artistically isolated in the city when so many of his fellow painters were enjoying the countryside, a decision made necessary by his deteriorating eyesight—an eyesight that he used to portray all the colors of the city from his disabled perch above it.

If Lyndon B. Johnson hadn't had his heart attack

Special thanks to Doris Kearns Goodwin's masterclass "U.S. Presidential History and Leadership" for the conceit of this poem.

Ursa Corregidora and Mary J. Blige Contemplate Life without Children

Special thanks to Jamie Broadnax for accepting my pitch to write on Mary J. Blige's documentary for Black Girl Nerds and to the conference organizers of the Gayl Jones Symposium—Tala Khanmalek, Kianna Middleton, and Ianna Hawkins Owen—for prompting me to write more about Corregidora.

Palimpsestina

I thought I was sooooo clever when I came up with this title, until I read *Owed*, by Joshua Bennett, which has a title by the same name. His sestina uses the end words *beast, black, forsythia, steel, hands*, and *left*. It takes a brave poet to choose *forsythia*. Bennett's "Palimpsestina" arrests the imagination because of the way the speaker employs the interlocking form of the sestina to write and rewrite both personal and national histories simultaneously. Taking advantage of the sestina form's leaning toward obsession, Bennett's poem turns the speaker's attention from inner visions (Stevie Wonder reference fully intended for its kaleidoscopic quality) to outward narratives that govern the Black body in the academy, on the street, anywhere we might live while in our glorious skin. As a result, the beast in question is both an ironic reference to the self and a deadly (emphasis on that) serious question; the forsythia blooms as a vibrant flowering hope in all instantiations of this history including the plea in the envoi: "forsythia/forsythia, make a world of these hands."

My own "Palimpsestina" starkly divides the sestet between two speakers struggling to communicate across the fraught time and space of dementia. I have refused some of the form's generosity by opting out of having one speaker, but I do seek the form's interest in "obsessive repetition" (*pace* Bob Hass) as a way to get to illness's tendency to write and rewrite all manner of (hi)stories.

What the palimpsestinas share is the impetus to acknowledge the present, write it, and write over it—to make concepts more messily imbricated rather than cleave them from each other. Both Bennett and I, steeped as we are in the traditions of Black writing, logophilia, and insatiable curiosity, would agree that the magical alchemy of poetry and feeling, writer and reader, can connive to open up another imaginative avenue.

Apostrophe to Inspiration

Originally, this was meant to be a palinode, inspired by Sally Wen Mao's *Mad Honey Symposium* (Alice James Books, 2014) and Stella Young's articulation of disability consciousness. As always, "inspiration" likes to take all the shine for itself.

Antony and Cleopatra, dir. Simon Godwin, National Theatre, 2019

Special thanks to Justin Shaw for his talk titled "Less Mad, More Sad: The Racial Politics of Melancholy in *Antony and Cleopatra*."

I Ain't Forget about Y'all; or Acknowledgments

I am humbled daily by my faith walk, the overwhelming love of the cross. I would rather have splinters near the foot of Calvary than smooth hands standing on my own. Thank You for paying a debt You didn't owe because we owed a debt we couldn't pay. This is the poetry of faith.

What had happened was, in 2013, Ken Wissoker heard me talk at the Conference of Ford Fellows and gave me his card. Mind you, that talk—which later turned into "What Drives Work: A Written Performance Piece"—was the hardest one I had ever written because it was the most deeply personal public statement I had ever given about disability, Blackness, womanhood, and being a professor. Ken heard the germ of the second book and traces of what would become this one. That serendipity never ceases to amaze me. Thank you, Ken! Special thanks to the Duke University Press editing team, including Kate Mullen, Liz Smith, and everyone who performed administrative labor, copyediting, and proofreading on this manuscript. Your labor is much appreciated!

Thank you to the principal funding sources for this project: Bates Faculty Development Fund, Phillips Fellowship, and my savings account. I appreciate my Bates colleagues for their willingness to financially and intellectually support my move to poetry. Special thanks to Myronn Hardy and Jessica Anthony for their encouragement and generosity about their own processes.

My early poetry professors saw a light in me that my own insecurity tried to extinguish: bless the minds and hearts of Yusef Komunyakaa and Harryette Mullen. Many of these poems were created in the context of community that freed my mind to be able to generate poems, and contemplate edits. Thank you to Margaret Porter Troupe Arts (2006), Community of Writers (2017 and 2020), Kenyon Review Poetry Workshop (2018), Colgate Writers' Workshop (2019), Bread Loaf—Sicily (2019), Hurston/Wright Virtual Workshop (2023), VONA Virtual Workshop (2023), and Rutgers University, Poets and Scholars Summer Writing Retreat (2023). Special thanks to the faculty: Quincy Troupe, Margaret Porter Troupe, Derek Walcott, Brenda Hillman, Gregory Pardlo, Forrest Gander, Robert Hass, Sharon Olds, Francisco Aragón, Carl Phillips, Eduardo Corral, Patrick Phillips, Ada Limón, Camille Dungy, Matthew Zapruder, Major Jackson, Imani Cezanne, Paisley Rekdal, and Cynthia Dewi Oka. I am immensely grateful to all the workshop participants in my groups. You all are magical. I deeply appreciate the community of The Grind: 100% accountability and 0% feedback. Thank you to my fellow grinders for putting up with my away message daily and sending fabulous poems.

Some folks read or listened and provided feedback on everything from the words to the lines, from the order to the emotional landscape. I appreciate your keen poetic eyes, your sharp wit, and your generosity in reading and/or listening: Amy Shimshon-Santo, Angela Siew, Ann Tweedy, Bettina Judd, Charif Shanahan, Eduardo Corral, El Williams, Hayan Charara, Herman Beavers, Joshua Bennett, Karen Llagas, Les James, Lydia T. Liu, Maria Gómez de Leon, Meta D. Jones, Myronn Hardy, Nate Marshall, Neema Avashia, Paisley Rekdal, Phil Metres, Phillip Barron, Rachel Myers, Tawanda Mulalu, and Yeva Johnson. Your sacrifice of time and energy buoyed me. The anonymous readers saw my work in a way that was incredibly powerful and affirming. Thank you for your generous words.

Making a transition between critical writing and poetry wasn't as seamless as I thought it would be. I am grateful for the folks who told me where to find community, how to trust my voice and my brain, how to navigate this new multihyphenate identity. So much of writing is listening and watching. You all reminded me that I can trust what my senses tell me. Bless you one-hundred-million-fold: Aria Halliday, Naomi Jackson, Bethel Kifle, Bettina Judd, Brandon Manning, Charif Shanahan, Erica Edwards, Evie Shockley, Gabriel Johnson, Gene Jarrett, Regina Bradley, Kiese Laymon, Jalen Baker, Jonathan Lee Walton, Leila Pazargadi, Michèlle Hartman, Michelle Wright, Moya Bailey, Nikki R. Brown, Richard Yarborough, Samuel K. Roberts, Stephen Engel, Rashonda Bailey, Farah Jasmine Griffin, Tonya Bailey Curry, Valerie Popp, and Willie Perdomo. I am deeply appreciative of my therapists (not named for privacy) for helping me renew my mind. Thank you to my physical trainer, Nicole Rush, who helped me listen to and trust my body. More thanks than ever to my vocal coach, Sharmayne Thomas, who helped me discover parts of my voice I didn't know were there.

Friendship is the gift of vulnerability, accountability, and companionship. Love to the only CCs I recognize: Courtney Baker and Courtney Marshall. Love to the people STAMPed on my heart: Shanna Benjamin, Shanique Brown, Timothy Lyle, Aaisha Tracy, Aria Halliday, Ayesha Hardison, Mara Casey Tieken, and Peyton Cyd Scott. You give me a safe space to land so I am free to create. You ask the hard questions. You are my soft shoulders, my avenging angels, my jaw-splitting comedians, and my sounding boards. I love you all more than all the words could possibly say.

My first storyteller: my mother, Lori A. Scott-Pickens. You taught me that every story has a beginning, a middle, and an end; that there's three sides to every story—yours, mine, and the truth; that a secret's not a secret if two people know it; and that "long story short" means we might be here for a while. Love you.

Thank you to those of you who are reading this. Thank you for your belief in the power of poetry, the magic of storytelling.

www.ingramcontent.com/pod-product-compliance
Lightning Source LLC
Chambersburg PA
CBHW080605170426
43196CB00017B/2907